COLD STEEL

by JOHN STYERS

Text prepared by Karl Schuon

Photographs by Louis Lowery

Cold Steel
Technique of Close Combat
by John Styers

Copyright © 1952 by John Styers

ISBN 0-87364-025-X
Printed in the United States of America

Published by Paladin Press, a division of
Paladin Enterprises, Inc., P.O. Box 1307,
Boulder, Colorado 80306, USA.
(303) 443-7250

Direct inquiries and/or orders to the above address.

Foreword

A sudden realization of the thorough preparation for combat which will become an integral part of a Marine recruit's life strikes grimly home when he arrives at Parris Island and reads its motto —"Let's be damned sure that no boy's ghost will ever say, 'If your training program had only done its job.'"

But that training program doesn't end with boot camp nor does it end as long as the man is a Marine. Training develops specialists, and every Marine is a fighting specialist, equipped with the knowledge necessary to qualify him for his important role on one of the world's deadliest teams. Wherever he may be, he is kept abreast of the warfare times, taught the battle techniques of tomorrow, and given confidence in his own proficiency—the proficiency of his Corps.

He is part of a team, trained to do his job in a coldly calculated war of scientific weapons and mass destruction. But the touted push button warfare has limitations, and they demand the individual's ability to meet his enemy face to face, steel to steel, hand to hand. Whether he is a radar operator, a communications man or a truck driver, he must be prepared to defend his own life in any eventuality. Close combat has been skillfully developed into a science of self-preservation—and the advance of death-dealing devices does not preclude the necessity for a basic knowledge of hand to hand principles and confidence in their application.

A Warning Word...

The publishers of *Cold Steel* wish to express their concern regarding the possible dangers involved in releasing a book of this type. It must be clearly understood that the principles prescribed on the following pages are intended to teach the fighting man to *kill*. Every precaution must be exercised in the practice of these principles; a slip in a careless attempt to perform movements described in this book may result in serious damage or the death of an innocent training partner. Care should be taken to prevent the book from falling into the hands of children who may thoughtlessly try some of these principles on their playmates. *Cold Steel* is a recipe for death; use it wisely!

PUBLISHER

Preface

Brutality makes apology impossible.

But as brutality begets cruelty, so apology begets explanation.

And, since America is not a brutal nation, the words between these covers are vulnerable to condemnation.

But an honest purpose cannot be damned. As long as other nations war against each other in lust, greed and ambition, brutality will persist and the brutal words on these pages will have a purpose.

When an atom bomb is loosed on a city, killing several hundred thousand people, the magnitude of suffering and death is incomprehensible to the average person and conjures up a picture of horror rather than brutality. If, however, the plane which dropped the bomb is forced down on enemy territory on the return flight, and the crew is faced with a hand-to-hand grapple with an enemy patrol where a hand throttling a throat, a knee smashing into a groin or a finger gouging an eye may mean life or death, then brutality becomes a reality.

The realness of brutality must be faced with the same direct approach in which we build an air raid shelter. World War II taught Americans the vast scope of atrocity; it would be criminal negligence to close our eyes to the bloody mayhem American military men will meet in the field. They must be taught to meet it with a basic knowledge of its principles, the practical application of those principles, and confidence in themselves to wage identical war.

To Americans, who fight fair and clean by heritage—when they can—we dedicate this book . . .

That they may save their own lives by confidently engaging their enemy with his own unprincipled principles.

Acknowledgments

The author is indebted to many people and organizations who were instrumental in broadening his knowledge and perspective of close combat technique. Grateful recognition is hereby accorded to those who have made this contribution.

The United States Marine Corps

The late Col. A. J. Drexel Biddle, USMCR

Col. William A. Kengla, USMC.·

Lt. Col. Walter R. Walsh, USMCR

Lt. Col. William E. Daly, Infantry, N. Y. Guard

George Santelli, Coach, American Olympic Fencing Team

Edward Lucia, 1st Assistant to Santelli

Sam Munson, Master of Arms, Sala Messineo

Carl Kitt, U.S. Naval Academy

Stephen V. Grancsay, The Metropolitan Museum of Art

Herbert Kreiger, Smithsonian Institute

Sylvester Vigilante, N. Y. Public Library

Robert Scott, Authority on James Bowie

General Leroy P. Hunt, USMC (Ret.)

Maj. General Ray A. Robinson, USMC

Mendel Peterson, Curator of Military and Naval History, Smithsonian Institute

And the many other individuals and organizations who have given generous cooperation and assistance.

Contents

The Bayonet

Part I

The Bayonet

For 300 years the use of the bayonet has remained the same; fundamentally it is a *pike*—its object:

To *stick* your opponent before he *sticks* you!

Let's face an opponent. Let's recognize the fact that he understands the use of his weapon, but let's not accept the supposition that the contest is going to be *even*. It doesn't have to be; *you* can have the advantage.

An aggressive opponent will thrust his bayonet at you, attempting to direct its point to the vital areas of your body—the chest or throat. This statement is ridiculously obvious, but it can be the basic action which will decide which one of you lives to engage another enemy. The *correct application* of the weapon in your hand will give you immediate command of the situation.

Merely knock your opponent's weapon aside and kill him!

Simply said. Simply done.

No fancy footwork; no intricate fencing, just two simple, natural movements combined with speed and accuracy.

The bayonet fighters of the old school will probably stop reading at this point and throw up their gnarled hands in rage, or shake their greying heads in pity, cynicism or wonder.

"Footwork and fencing," they will insist, "are the foundations on which bayonet fighting is built!"

No one will discount the value of these two fine aspects of bayonet technique, but their value was based on the one great doubt which has always haunted bayonet wielders:

"On which side of my blade will my opponent's blade fall? My correct parry depends upon where his blade falls."

True.

But this doubt can be eliminated by furnishing your opponent with ONLY ONE TARGET. The position in which you hold *your* piece

1

will determine the direction of his weapon; you know where it *will be;* when it comes within your range, one deft move of your body will remove instantly the target he thought he had. In its place he will find your blade, pointed directly at his throat—his own weapon sawing the thin air.

YOUR thrust ends the engagement.

THE GUARD POSITION

The text and photographs in this book are intended for RIGHT-HANDED persons. Individuals who are LEFT-HANDED will simply REVERSE the directions given.

The Body

In learning to assume the *guard position,* the following steps will prove helpful:

1. Stand at attention at port arms.
2. Turn the piece AWAY from you, placing the blade OUTBOARD.

The proper hold on the piece at port arms. The blade faces
outboard. This is the first step in learning the guard position

3

From port arms drop into a guard position. The body should be well balanced in a crouch with the feet placed diagonally

3. Release your *left hand* from the proper port arms hold and regrasp the piece on the *upper hand guard,* immediately *above* the upper sling swivel.

4. Now, WITHOUT MOVING THE POSITION OF THE ARMS, assume the boxer's crouch, high or low as the occasion may demand. Remember that the point should be to the left, but on a level with your opponent's eyes.

4

The Blade

The edge of the blade must be kept on line with the forearm. In this position the cutting edge will be ready for use with no loss of time or effort. In addition, your blade will have greater strength when striking your opponent's piece, if the blow is made with the blade held vertical to the striking surface, rather than in a flat position. It means the difference between one vertical inch of steel and one quarter of an inch if the blade strikes with its flat surface.

The Hands

The *left hand* grasps the upper hand guard and *remains there* except when it is released to execute the "Throw Point".

The fingers of the *right hand* are securely wrapped around the *small* of the stock.

The Feet

The body is well-balanced—feet apart at an angle, left foot in *front* of the right.

The Piece

The piece is held at an *angle* exposing the upper torso on the *right* of the blade.

All formidable attacks can be made from the guard position. You can walk or run with this guard just as you would with your rifle held at port. With a mere movement of your body you can drop instantly into guard and engage an enemy. Briefly, in this position, you are *always* "ON GUARD".

THE BEAT THRUST

This simple movement is the *meat* of all your attacks.

The moment your opponent's blade comes within your range, close the gap and at the same time, with the full weight of your body, beat his blade with a severe rap, and immediately *thrust* home.

5

The point of your blade will drop slightly with the motion, coming into line with your opponent's upper chest or throat. There will be a tendency, at first, to overshoot your *beat;* this means that your point will have gone too far over to line up on your opponent's throat. This lack of control is to be expected at first, simply because you will be overly anxious to assure yourself that his blade is absolutely knocked aside. If this happens, it will mean that you will have to *recover* by whipping your blade back, cutting the side of your opponent's head or neck. If possible, whip the blade back into line with your opponent's throat or chest—and thrust. Recovery of your blade back into line for a thrust depends upon the agility of your opponent; if he is too slow to take advantage of your overshot beat with a Butt Stroke, you will have time to line up your blade. "Time", in this instance, refers to fractions of seconds, and what you do with eight-tenths of a second may mean the difference between a Stateside liberty and a clipped dog tag.

The Beat

It is NOT difficult to beat your enemy's blade aside before thrusting. Here's proof:

Select the strongest man available; give him a rifle and scabbarded bayonet; have him assume the *usual* guard position.

Now take your index finger and attempt to move his blade. YOU WILL BE ABLE TO MOVE HIM IN A COMPLETE CIRCLE! If you can do this with your finger you can most certainly do it with your blade!

Attack Your Opponent's Blade

The length of your enemy's weapon is unimportant. Actually, the longer your opponent's weapon is, the easier it will be for you to beat it aside—YOU ATTACK HIS *BLADE!*

The Carbine?

If you are carrying a short carbine it will protect your vital chest and throat areas if you use the prescribed guard. It is equally as effective as a larger weapon.

Pivot your body and beat. When executing this movement you
will be wheeling the blade's point into line with the opponent

7

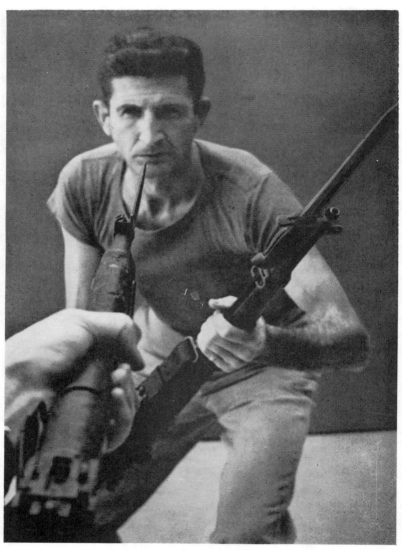

The guard position before the beat. Your opponent has only
one target; he is forced to attack on the right of your blade

The beat. Your blade should be in a vertical position when it strikes the opponent's weapon. Follow immediately with thrust

9

The side view of the beat from the guard position. The blade
is held broadside for strength when striking enemy's weapon

10

The thrust. Your left arm is extended fully as your weapon travels forward in a fast, powerful drive, directly to a target

11

You know where to expect your opponent's attack. When the enemy's weapon comes into range you are prepared to beat

Your first contact should be made with the opponent's blade.
Do not overshoot beat or point will not line up on opponent

13

The fingers on the left hand may be opened on thrust. Your
piece, grasped by the right fingers, is powered by right arm

14

THE THROW POINT

When you find an exposed target, for example, if your opponent drops his blade too low for you to successfully beat it aside, SNAP THE WHOLE WEAPON FORWARD with the full power of the right arm, the *right hand* grasping the *small* of the stock. The piece is guided to the enemy's throat or chest by the *left hand* which releases its grip, allowing the piece to be extended. RECOVER IMMEDIATELY TO THE GUARD POSITION.

You will find the Throw Point effective in nailing opponents on the run. In a chase, your enemy may escape unless you take advantage of the added reach provided by the Throw Point. USE IT QUICKLY!

The long throw point should not be attempted unless you are armed with a carbine. The left arm thrown back adds power

15

Throw point with carbine to the head. The weapon is guided to target by left hand. The right hand grasps small of stock

Throw point with M-1. Movement can be accomplished either without a beat or after a beat. Open left hand guides weapon

THE HAND CUT

Bayonet fighting is deeply indebted to the science of sword play for many tricks of its trade. The effective Hand Cut, relatively unknown by other nations, is a valuable carry-over from sword fighting. The Hand Cut is directed at your opponent's left hand which is extended, supporting the piece. DO NOT ATTEMPT TO USE THE POINT, instead, the cutting edge of the blade is brought down on the enemy's left hand—lobbing off as many fingers as possible. A crippled opponent is easy prey for a final thrust.

The Throw Point can be used effectively in the Hand Cut but in most instances a Beat Cut will be more accurate and decisive.

Throw point to opponent's extended hand in attempt to make a hand cut. Left step simultaneously accompanies this action

17

Close up of the hand cut. You will gain an early advantage if your cut is successful

The hand cut with the carbine. Glide your blade down along
the side of your enemy's front hand guard, chopping fingers

THE BUTT STROKE

The BLADE is more deadly than the BUTT, and most Butt Strokes
leave the blade facing in the opposite direction of the target. However,
ONE Butt Stroke IS prescribed.

Remember that your rifle is primarily a SHOOTING weapon, and,
as such, it should be valued. A man should come out of a bayonet
engagement with blood on his blade, and his rifle in perfect condition.

Butt Strokes can easily reduce your piece to kindling wood.

The Prescribed Butt Stroke

This stroke follows an *unsuccessful* Beat Thrust, PROVIDED YOUR OPPONENT HAS BLOCKED THE COMPLETION OF YOUR THRUST by forcing your blade UPWARD with his piece.

When your opponent's piece is in this position it is impossible for him to protect his GROIN—that's where you plant a hard, direct Butt Stroke immediately. The blow, if well placed, will eliminate any further resistance from your opponent, and the softness of that area of his body cannot damage your weapon.

If an opponent blocks your thrust this way he will be unable to protect lower region of his body. Step in with rear foot

If it is impossible for you to use the point of the blade, stoop and smash your opponent's groin with prescribed butt stroke

After butt stroke lower body and spring with a short jab

If thrust fails, hand cut will block opponent's butt stroke

21

LOCKED PIECES

If your Beat parry is unsuccessful and results in locking pieces with your opponent, TRY THE PRESCRIBED *BUTT STROKE*. If a Butt Stroke is impossible TRY FOR A *HAND CUT*.

If your pieces are locked on your *right* you have the following alternatives:

1. Bounce your blade repeatedly against the enemy's blade and work your blade into a position from which you can tilt your weapon and slice or chop off his fingers.

When your beat fails, locked pieces will result. Bounce your blade on his weapon until you are ready to try for hand cut

2. Release your pressure on his blade slightly, enough to enable you to guide his blade over to your left; then QUICKLY release the pressure entirely, whipping your blade around and into position for a Thrust, Hand Cut or Head Cut. The choice is yours because you are on his LEFT SIDE—his *weakest* and most *vulnerable* side. His whole left arm is yours if you want it; chop it with the cutting edge of your blade or bring your blade across the side of his head.

Release the pressure on your opponent's blade until you are able to maneuver it to a harmless position on your left side

23

3. Close in tight and drop down, bringing the pieces in close to you; then work the point back and forth with your arms and body in a swinging or up and down motion. KEEP YOUR ARMS LOCKED: the motion should come from your legs and body. Your hands need not change their position on the piece. You can hug the weapon as closely as you wish with the "GUARD" hold.

After his blade has cleared your head, disengage your piece abruptly and whip it around. Try for hand, arm or head cut

4. Don't forget that you have two heavily-shod feet. USE THEM TO CRUSH YOUR OPPONENT'S FOUNDATION—his instep, shin bone or knee. USE YOUR OWN KNEES, they are excellent battering rams—very effective when brought up swiftly and solidly into your opponent's groin.

Following your cut, drop into a position for a short jab. Full leg action will provide the jab with an additional power drive

25

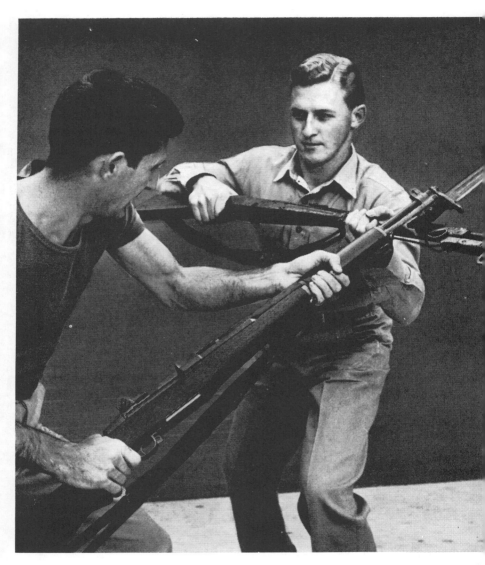

If you have overshot your beat and the weapons are locked
on the right, bounce your piece into position for a head cut

If you find that your blade is out of line on your opponent's
left side, whip the piece back into his throat or side of head

27

TARGETS

Your targets in bayonet fighting are, of course, any targets you can hit, but there *is* a *preferable* target. One thrust of only three inches of blade in the THROAT or CENTER CHEST area will abruptly end that particular personal engagement. The major veins and arteries are bunched, practically unprotected, in these two areas. They are fairly close to the surface, therefore, more easily severed than in other portions of the body.

Place your fist on your chest, between the left nipple and the center breast bone; this is the location of your heart which is just about the size of your fist.

Above the heart lies the largest artery of the body. From this artery, which is as thick as a garden hose, spring numerous smaller arteries.

Along both sides of the windpipe are large arteries which supply the blood being pumped to the head. Their pulsation can be felt by placing the fingers on each side of the windpipe and applying slight pressure.

The neck area contains in addition, four large jugular veins which carry the blood down from the head.

The spine is the only bone in the neck but it is located in the rear, leaving the front of the throat vulnerable to attack—and an instantly fatal target for a thrust or cut.

In spite of all the speculation about the blade becoming lodged or catching the bone when it is thrust into the chest area, YOUR BLADE WILL *NOT* GET CAUGHT IN A BONE! The framework in that area is composed mostly of cartilage; the small percentage of bone in that portion of the body is very thin. It takes little effort to thrust through. DON'T thrust through to the shoulder blades.

THE IN-QUARTATA OR OUT OF LINE

This is the only prescribed movement which is purely *defensive*. It is used most effectively against any running attack coming in your direction.

Wait, or halt momentarily in the guard position, until your opponent comes within range. At this moment, snap your whole body to your *left*, pivoting on the *left* foot, propelled by a thrust with your *right* leg which, crosses behind the left foot.

Your spin has removed your whole body from the line of your enemy's attack. HE WILL MISS YOU BY ABOUT THREE FEET. As you spin, the point of your piece will swing into direct line with your opponent's attack. You may thrust or just leave your blade there; the momentum of his attack will force him to run into it.

If your opponent rushes you in a wild plunge, instantly snap
to the guard position in a direct line with his headlong attack

30

The instant that your opponent comes into range execute the beat and, at the same time, propel body to left with rear foot

31

As you execute the full beat, your body, well balanced on the forward foot, will pivot out of line with your opponent's attack

You have removed yourself from your enemy's line of attack.
Execute a full thrust into his onrushing body as it passes you

33

YELLING

The value of YELLING when making an attack cannot be over-emphasized. A lusty shout at the right moment can distract your opponent, momentarily paralyzing his ability to think. It is an established fact that yelling will harden the muscles of your stomach and chest, increasing the power of your attack.

THE VOLT

Pivoting to change direction is called VOLTING.

LEAP into the air and land in the desired direction at the guard position. Practice will make your VOLT simple, fast and effective.

NOTES

SHOOT if you can.

DON'T get "POSE HAPPY" in learning the technique of the bayonet. Master the fundamental principles and learn to execute them efficiently.

RELAX. Remain at ease; avoid stiffness. Keep your mind and body functioning smoothly and alertly by sizing up the situation and making quick decisions. Knowing what to do, and when to do it will eliminate dangerous tension.

Practice PULLING YOUR PUNCH when you Beat. Beat vigorously but STOP when your point is LINED UP with your opponent's throat or chest.

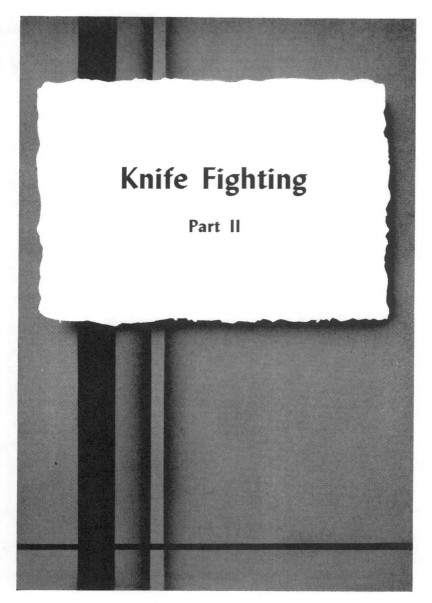

Knife Fighting

Part II

Knife Fighting

The sight of sharp, cold steel in your enemy's hand is not a pleasant sight. Knife fighting is an ugly business; it means steel against steel; then steel against flesh—and death.

Let's take a look at your enemy's blood.

That's one thing you can't draw from the quartermaster by signing a chit.

But it's a lot easier to draw than size 13 boondockers—you know that your enemy has it . . .

You're far behind the lines, maybe you're a communications man operating your switchboard. Your carbine is propped against a tree nearby. Your outfit is in the area but out of sight. You're alone, and you're intent on your job.

You've been warned that there is the possibility of guerrilla activity and infiltration. Your knife is constantly at your side. It gives you a great deal of confidence, but your real assurance comes from your confidence in your own ability to save your own life with that knife by carving out a heavenly military career for your enemy in whatever particular Valhalla he happens to believe exists.

A twig snaps!

You look up from the switchboard.

An enemy is rushing at you, both hands raised—in each a knife! He's got one objective:

To drive them downward into your chest!

"MOVE, BOY!"

You move. You whip up your knife; you leap into the guard position. Your enemy slows his advance; immediately he realizes that before him is no frightened schoolboy. Instead, he sees a calm, fighting man—poised, ready for instantaneous action, armed with deadly steel, its point directed menacingly at his throat.

You advance cautiously into your proper range, your knife never wavering from his throat. Both of his fists are out in front of him. They are your first targets.

Too late, he realizes that your range is greater than his, and that he has allowed you to come in too close. Like the fangs of a cobra your blade strikes out in a full cut and you are back in your guard position, your blade again pointed at his throat.

There is a dull thud on the ground and a mild ping as the knife falls from your opponent's left hand, along with parts of his fingers if your cut has been accurate and hard.

You have stunned your opponent; you can afford a split second before pressing the attack. From your guard position you lower yourself quickly, and with your blade still pointed at his throat, you scoop up a handful of dirt and return to the guard position.

You are ready for the kill. Your enemy is now in a do or die rage; his only thought is to kill YOU any way he can. He raises his blade beside his head and charges.

You heave the dirt, execute an *in-quartata,* and yell. Your target is his heart.

As he hurtles by the spot you vacated a moment before, your blade is almost wrenched from your hand as it cuts its way out of his body.

Your opponent is now lying about five yards beyond the spot in which he had intended to leave YOUR lifeless form.

Cautiously you inspect the corpse of your enemy. Your job was clean. There was no need for in-fighting.

"Just like that?" you ask cynically.

We nod.

"But that wasn't *me* in that knife fight," you insist. "It must have been some other guy, an expert, maybe . . ."

You don't need to be an expert to stand your ground in the guard position and engage an enemy with confidence. A sound KNOWLEDGE of knife fighting and PRACTICE of its basic PRINCIPLES will make you a dangerous opponent for any knife-wielding enemy.

Knife fighting is based on the age-old science of swordsmanship. These principles of swordplay were utilized by James Bowie in his fine technique with his Bowie knife—making Bowie and the Bowie Knife one of the deadliest blade combinations the world has ever known.

38

HOLDING THE KNIFE

Here, take this knife.

Now, hold it straight, NOT cocked upward. Put your thumb directly on top of the handle, on the SAME side as the FLAT EDGE of the blade—that's right, the cutting edge faces DOWNWARD.

Now, clamp the fingers securely UPWARD around the handle. Lock your wrist when the ELBOW and the POINT of the knife are in a STRAIGHT LINE. THE KNIFE IS MERELY AN EXTENSION OF THE FOREARM.

Keep the thumb about a quarter of an inch from the thumb guard. This space is allowed to take up the shock caused by the impact when your knife strikes its target.

Tips

1. Keep the wrist LOCKED at all times.
2. DON'T arch the thumb on the thumb guard.
3. Keep the blade ON LINE with the FOREARM.

The hold. Fingers are wrapped securely around the handle, thumb on top, point of your blade is on a line with the elbow

39

THE STANCE

The proper fighting GUARD position is taken directly from the stance of the skilled swordsman. There are only two changes. These changes are made, *only when learning*, after the proper SABRE STANCE has been assumed. In actual combat you snap IMMEDIATELY into the KNIFE FIGHTING GUARD POSITION.

The Sabre Stance

1. Face your opponent at attention.
2. Execute a LEFT FACE.
3. Execute a "close interval DRESS RIGHT." (Glance at your opponent, placing the left hand on the hip at the same time.)
4. Point your RIGHT FOOT at your opponent and advance it about TWO FEET in his direction.
5. Raise your RIGHT FOREARM, aiming the point of your knife directly at your opponent's throat. Your ELBOW will be approximately six inches forward from your HIP.
6. The knees are slightly bent until the lower part of the RIGHT LEG is straight up and down—ready for instantaneous advance or withdrawal.
7. The CUTTING EDGE of the blade should be facing DOWN and to the RIGHT in an unstrained, natural position.
8. YOUR WRIST IS LOCKED.
9. Keep the upper part of the body ERECT at all times.

This is the proper SABRE STANCE. Notice how easily you are able to *advance* and *withdraw—forward* and *backward*. Movement to the left or right is more difficult.

In practice, a *knife, bayonet* or *stick* may represent the sabre.

To assume the knife duelist stance
from the sabre stance

1. Assume that there is a STRAIGHT LINE between you and your opponent. Move your REAR foot from one to two feet LEFT of this line, forming a 90 degree angle to your opponent with your feet. IN THIS POSITION YOU HAVE COMPLETE STABILITY. You can

The sabre stance, foundation
for the knife fighter's stance

Sabre stance to knife fighter
stance. Move rear foot to left

The guard position. Left arm
free. Knife arm drawn back

The thrust. Blade drives into
target. Free arm snaps back

propel yourself easily and quickly either BACKWARD or FORWARD or to the LEFT or RIGHT.

2. Draw the arm which holds the knife BACK, CLOSE TO THE BODY and, at the same time, square your shoulders to your opponent. In sabre fighting the arm can be safely extended because the weapon is long and the handle is equipped with a hand guard. In knife fighting you have a lightning-fast blade but there is little protection for the hand.

3. The LEFT ARM swings FREE of the body.

Your body should be relaxed WITH THE EXCEPTION of the LOCKED WRIST and the THIGHS which are taut because of the bent knees.

Your shoulders face your opponent squarely. In this position there will be no lead with your shoulder and knife betraying the nature of your attack.

The guard position *will* become a natural reaction. Place a sabre or a rapier in the hand of an experienced duelist and he will immediately snap into the guard position with a reflex action almost as strong as drawing the hand from a hot surface. This may be difficult to understand at first, but be assured, *it is true* and after a moderate amount of knife-fighting practice, you'll find yourself assuming the guard position without thinking about it, the moment you have a knife in your hand.

Tips

1. Keep your feet at about a 90 degree angle.

2. The blade is drawn in, close to the body, and held in an unbroken line from your elbow to the point.

3. Shoulders face the opponent squarely.

4. Torso and head are held erect.

5. The arm on hip should swing free, but care must be taken to prevent it from extending beyond the hand which holds the knife.

6. Your blade points directly at your opponent's throat.

PRACTICE all the points of the proper stance until you can draw your blade on command of "On Guard!" and instantaneously snap into the perfect position without losing a second to make major adjustments.

The side view of the guard position. Major portions of the body will not be extended into an opponent's range

The straight thrust, side view. The torso pivots on axis of spine. Your legs provide added range

PRACTICE until ALL of the points in the ON GUARD position become coordinated into ONE natural movement.

ALL OF THE ATTACKS AND DEFENSES OF THE SKILLED KNIFE FIGHTER ORIGINATE FROM THIS GUARD POSITION.

THE THRUST

From the guard position, the blade is thrust forward with explosive force DIRECTLY at the target. The free arm is whipped back to add power and velocity to this POINT-AT-TARGET attack.

The BLADE POINT travels straight to the TARGET, backed by the full power of the forearm and shoulder.

The THRUST starts with the knife, poised and ready in the guard position. NO PRELIMINARY MOVEMENT IS NECESSARY. The blade is snapped directly to the target. If the target is your opponent's throat your point should strike in a direct line to the throat.

On the thrust, the free arm has been whipped back, TURNING THE FULL BODY WITH A SNAP. Instead of the full spread of the shoulders and chest which *had* been exposed to your opponent, you now present the NARROWEST view of your body. The upper portion of the body has pivoted forming a straight line from your blade point back along your arm, across the shoulders and down the free arm in the rear.

In executing the thrust, the beginner will have a tendency to lean forward and *push*. The result of a push is usually an UNEVEN and weak action. Your attack should be instantaneous. From the front, your opponent should see only the blur of a point on the extended arm, and the sudden disappearance of the broadside view of your upper body; in its place, your enemy will find only the thin silhouette of the NARROWEST portion of the torso.

The attitude of your blade, well back and pointed at your opponent's throat, is like a pistol leveled at a target—ammo in the chamber, the hammer back, your finger on the trigger. The *point* is your *bullet*.

THE THRUST, when properly executed with your opponent within range, will be so swift that he'll never see it.

He won't know what hit him.

He won't see it coming.

Nor can he PREVENT getting HIT.

This is true in professional boxing. If an opponent is *open* and *in range* of a left jab, he's going to be *hit*.

If an opponent tries to make an underhanded attack he will come within your range but you will still be out of his reach

Your advantage over your opponent is a range of eighteen to twenty-four inches. If the enemy attacks, he comes into range

The only way to avoid getting hit is NOT to be THERE to get hit. Simply said. Simply explained—later. But here's a hint:

DISTANCE is of utmost importance. It is INSURANCE against NOT being THERE to get hit, AND STILL BEING IN A POSITION TO run your opponent through.

Tips

1. When THE THRUST is executed in *practice* and the blade is not driven into human flesh; the blade completes its thrust in *mid air* where it stops abruptly with a NATURAL WHIPPING ACTION.

It is the conviction of the writer that the Bowie-shaped blade was

If your opponent tries an overhand stroke he must come in close; your straight thrust pivots your chest out of his range

46

scientifically designed by James Bowie for the control of this natural whip.

2. The THRUSTING HAND, when fully extended, should have the KNUCKLES UP, the THUMB LEFT and the knife arching *slightly downward* into the target. The FULL thrust is executed regardless of your opponent's distance—as long as he is IN RANGE.

3. Do not be too anxious to draw the weapon back prematurely. Let the extended arm SNAP OUT TO THE FULLEST.

4. Only in a well-executed thrust which does NOT strike home, will you find the whip-like movement of the blade. When the point reaches its target, penetrating flesh or bone, the whip is taken up by the substance which is hit.

An enemy's overhand stroke leaves him wide open for your thrust. He can be stopped before he reaches effective range

THE CUT

The thrust is the foundation of the CUT. With the thrust you take your knife to the target. If a FULL thrust does not strike the target the natural whipping action will take place. This whip is THE CUT.

The Vertical Cut

The VERTICAL CUT is a thrust which ends abruptly with the THUMB UP, the NAILS to the LEFT.

When this thrusting cut goes straight to its target instead of ending in mid-air, this same whipping action will take place

48

The vertical cut—fast and effective
for a long range slash. Whip down

The natural whipping action of the
thrusting cut makes the blade drop

49

An extended extremity, such as a protruding arm, is an excellent target for the VERTICAL CUT. In this cut the blade flashes DOWN and UP, biting gashes into the flesh or lobbing off fingers. The blade, when executing this action does not only whip DOWN and UP, but when it is viewed from the side, the observer will notice that it also RIPS FORWARD. Where a stiletto or narrow pointed knife would penetrate like an ice pick and leave a puncture wound, the Bowie-shaped blade will whip down into the target, ride forward, then snap UP.

THIS IS ONE CONTINUOUS ACTION. The movement has been completed in one ninety-fourth of a second when recorded by a high-speed camera.

All tissues, muscles, veins or tendons caught in the path of the scimitar-like hook of the Bowie blade will be sliced clean through.

Keep full thrust's distance from opponent's nearest extremity.
If nearest target is hand or forearm, execute a thrusting cut

The vertical thrusting cut to the hand. The blade is cocked in preparation for a wrist action to supplement the natural whip

Vertical thrusting cut ends with the blade biting down, ripping forward, then snapping up again—all in a continuous action

The Horizontal Cut

The HORIZONTAL CUT, *straight across and back,* is purely an unfulfilled normal thrust.

The tendency of the average knife fighter to *crouch* usually places his *head* and *face* in such a position that they present excellent targets for the HORIZONTAL CUT.

The horizontal thrusting cut. A full thrust is directed to right side of your target. Slightly cocked blade assists whip action

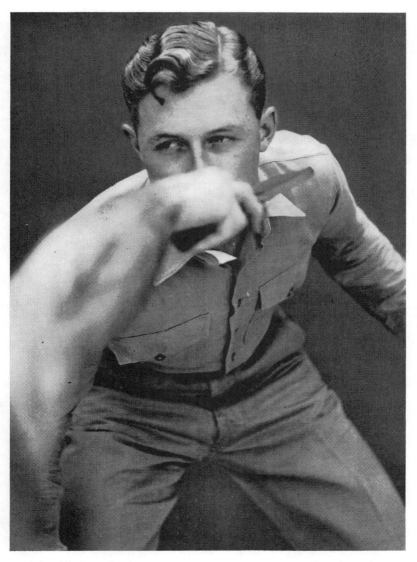

The blade will whip across its target automatically when the
arm is fully extended. Try for cuts on enemy's head or face

The finish of your horizontal thrusting cut. The blade whips back across target, achieving two cuts with only one thrust

The Hand Cut

The HAND CUT can be an exquisitely executed attack. From the hand of a skilled knife duelist this cut, practically unknown to the overhand or underhand knife fighter, can usually be relied upon to effectively strike the first blow. A deeply sliced hand will greatly reduce the strength of your opponent's knife hand, but if you hack off a few fingers with your initial HAND CUT you have it made!

Practice

These cuts may be practiced with an actual or simulated weapon, but when learning, the use of the hand in lieu of the weapon is advised. Master the whip of the HAND and you will develop a better understanding of the action of the blade.

When the hand alone is used, the fingers should be extended and joined; the edge of the hand opposite the thumb becomes the imaginary cutting edge of the knife. The hand is thrust out vigorously, coming to an abrupt halt at the fullest extension of the arm. A whip-like snap of the hand will take place. This practice will be valuable if you are ever confronted by an opponent when you are unarmed. for the edge of the hand, in this position, is used like an axe; the fingers joined at the tip are like the point of a blade.

After mastering the cut *as directed*, you may then increase the effectiveness of the blade by a snapping WRIST action in a whip-like manner, directing the cutting edge of your blade to its target with greater velocity. This sharp wrist-snapping cut is of utmost importance when the target is so close that it must be reached without fully extending your arm.

Tips

1. When learning the full extended cut, which is a result of the unfulfilled thrust, there will be a marked tendency to assist the action with wrist movement. AVOID THIS WHEN LEARNING. The cut is a completely natural action of the arm. *Later* when you understand this natural action, you may add additional wrist action to supplement the natural whip.

2. Draw the blade back to the guard position immediately *after* the cut is made.

3. Keep the blade pointed at the throat at all times except when making definite attacks to other targets.

4. Practice executing the full VERTICAL and HORIZONTAL CUT until the action is clean. The blade must avoid making circles at the full extension of the arm. These circles are the result of forced action of the wrist or forearm, preventing the NATURAL ACTION of the blade.

5. Begin your practice with the hand so that you may better understand and control the whip action.

6. Continue your practice until you work out the stiffness in the elbow joint. The tendons in this area will feel the strain while you're learning the thrust and cut.

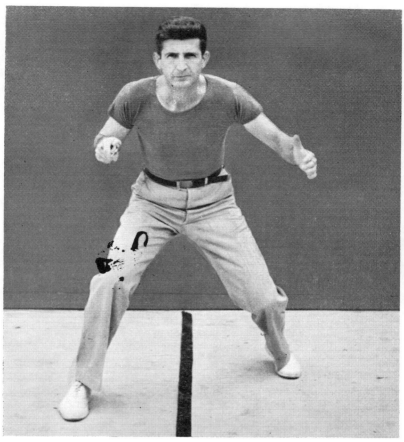

The in-quartata or out-of-line starts from the guard position.
Conceal the nature of your attack until opponent is in range

IN-QUARTATA OR OUT-OF-LINE

The defensive movement in fencing known as in-quartata or OUT-OF-LINE is a fine movement of the feet which throws the body approximately three feet out of the line of your opponent's attack if he attacks with so much force that you do not choose to be there to meet it with a stop thrust.

From your guard position, knees slightly bent, you execute a full thrust as the torso vigorously pivots, assisted by the free arm whipping

When opponent rushes into range, thrust home and apply
power with the rear leg, directing the body to the right side

back. You will also utilize the FULL POWER of your REAR leg to
pivot the whole body on the FORWARD leg. Your rear leg swings
around in an arc and lands on the opposite side. Your entire stance
should now look like a full sabre thrust from a sabre stance, but YOU
ARE AT AN ANGLE TO YOUR OPPONENT.

Your opponent's momentum will carry him over your original position, by about two or three feet. There will be no need for you to
withdraw your blade from your opponent, his momentum will carry
his BODY OUT OF THE BLADE!

Your rear leg will push off and swing to the right, pivoting
the body out of line with the oncoming rush of your opponent

The full pivot out of line, with your rear foot solidly planted.
Retain your full thrust, letting the opponent cut the blade out

If you attack an enemy from the rear or flank, try a straight
thrust to the throat with the full edge, not the point, of your
blade. Immediately draw the knife back, snapping the cutting
edge of the knife across opponent's throat, making two cuts

DISTANCE

Now we're going to try to clear up some of those doubts in your mind.

Sure, your opponent's got a knife—maybe he's got two knives.

And maybe he knows how to use them.

But, here and now, we want to cut you in on a big slice of scoop— IF YOU'VE GOT A *BOWIE KNIFE* IN YOUR HAND you're armed with a BETTER WEAPON than any other nation in the world has ever devised.

And that's only half the scoop. A KNOWLEDGE of the BASIC PRINCIPLES of the use of the Bowie knife or ANY BLADE simply means that you'll be able to save your blood for a Stateside blood bank instead of leaving it on the battlefield.

Up to this point you've learned three basic principles:

THE GUARD POSITION.

THE THRUST.

THE CUT.

"All of this," you will say, "is fine on the drill field or in a gym, but what do I do when I'm in combat and a crazy enemy comes chargin' at me with a wicked lookin' dagger? The guy's gonna kill me if I don't do something to stop him!"

You're right. He'll kill you if you don't do something immediately to discourage him.

CONFIDENCE in YOURSELF is your primary MENTAL attack. A bucketful of his wild zest will drain from him when he sees you plant yourself in the guard position and DEFY him. He'll stop in his tracks and think things over. You have won part of the mental duel, but the physical bout has just begun.

SIZE UP YOUR OPPONENT.

You will be able to judge the EFFECTIVE RANGE of your opponent immediately by the way he holds his blade and the stance he takes.

If your opponent has his blade in his RIGHT hand and has his LEFT foot forward, he will telegraph his attack with a body movement, even if he holds the blade in the *sabre manner.*

If he holds the blade in the OVERHAND or UNDERHAND position, or in any position other than that of a *sabre,* he will definitely LIMIT

(A) Keep yourself out of range of your opponent's full thrust.
If he attacks, you'll be forcing him to come into your range

the effectiveness of his RANGE. This is the predominant stance of most knife fighters throughout the world in spite of the fact that it is contrary to the 400-year-old fencing principle of keeping the RIGHT FOOT FORWARD.

If he extends his knife-holding hand to any marked degree, regardless of his grip, he is also LIMITING his range.

With practice, you will IMMEDIATELY notice these errors in your opponent and TAKE ADVANTAGE OF THEM.

If you are confronted by an opponent who displays these errors, the rule is simple:

STAY ONE FULL THRUST'S DISTANCE AWAY FROM YOUR OPPONENT'S NEAREST EXTREMITY.

From this range you will be in a position to continually SNIPE at him with LIGHTNING-LIKE cuts. You will be amazed to find that,

(B) Above picture shows your opponent in the same position as in (A) on opposite page, but you have been able to advance

although he is in range of getting cut by your blade, he cannot try for a cut on you without missing by ONE or TWO FEET.

If your opponent should BODILY ADVANCE in an attack, MAKE IMMEDIATE USE OF YOUR LEGS: they are slightly bent in the guard position and ready for instantaneous action. If your enemy's advance is slow, you merely STEP BACK—REAR foot FIRST, followed by the FORWARD foot.

If you are pressing the attack and are advancing, your first step will be made by the FORWARD foot; bring the REAR foot up BEFORE taking a second step with the FORWARD foot.

If your opponent assumes a skilled knife duelist's stance you will recognize it immediately—AND BECOME EXTREMELY CAUTIOUS. He will be OUT OF RANGE. You will have NO immediate TARGET, and you will have to work hard to GET one.

The slightest extension of your opponent's knife hand presents
a target. Strike and recover immediately to a guard position

With THIS opponent:

1. Your DISTANCE will be INCREASED. Stay one full thrust's
distance from *his* full thrust's distance. The distance is from HAND
to HAND. Your blade fully extended to his hand; his blade fully
extended to your hand.

2. Usually the HANDS will be your targets.

3. The duel is on, and you will have to resort to fencing TECH-
NIQUES to draw him into your range.

4. Attack your opponent when he is LEAST alert to your attack.
When you sense that HE is about to attack, he will be thinking of
HIS OWN strategy—NOT of his own defense.

Draw your opponent into an attack but keep your body in a
well-balanced position and out of opponent's striking distance

5. You may wish to attack when your opponent is IN MOTION—
EXECUTING an attack or RETURNING from one. In this moment,
his LACK OF BALANCE and the DISTANCE will be definitely IN
YOUR FAVOR. Once you have launched your attack, catching your
opponent off balance, force your attack with straight thrusts and cuts.

DISTANCE and TIMING are closely allied; *distance* is a matter of
keeping within a safe defensive range, and at the same time, being
within an effective offensive range. *Timing* is something you will
always have to FEEL; it is the ability to recognize the proper moment
to attack.

If your hand is too close to opponent's knife for a thrusting cut, try for a sabre cut—a full, snapping chop at knife hand

TECHNIQUE

Technique is the ability to combine basic principles with their best possible application to make the most skillful and formidable attacks against an opponent. Crudely put, it is the use of every trick you know to get your blade into your opponent.

Technique is NOT a sometimes thing; you acquire it with the PRACTICE of BASIC PRINCIPLES, in your own, individual manner.

It will PAY OFF in blood on YOUR blade . . .

TARGETS

After the fight you'll probably want to wipe off your blade. But if you don't hit anything you won't have to clean it; as a matter of fact, if you don't hit anything, your opponent probably will and what he hits will be PART OF YOU.

LOOK for targets on HIM, and let them feel your steel. IN A KNIFE DUEL, ANY TARGET IS A GOOD ONE TO BEGIN. THE KILL, HOWEVER, IS THE ULTIMATE.

Here are your targets:

1. The *hand* that holds his blade.
2. The *heart* which pumps his blood.
3. The *throat* which contains his windpipe and blood supply to and from his head.
4. His *chest area* which contains his lungs, heart, diaphragm and various other things he'd rather not have punctured.
5. His *back*, below the shoulder blades. Thrust the knife INBOARD, toward the center of his body. Work your knife handle back and forth; this will do far more damage than a single thrust. In any portion of the back, chest, stomach or throat area PUMP THE HANDLE OF YOUR KNIFE.

For an enemy attack, feint a low attack; draw his weapon low

When the opponent lowers his blade, attack his hand or wrist

Whip the blade up for a thrusting cut to your opponent's head

Attempt a straight thrust for your opponent's head or throat

69

Passata sotto, an alternative for out-of-line. If your opponent rushes with exposed lower right side, thrust to lower chest

PASSATA SOTTO

Another means of getting your blade into your opponent, other than the direct manner from the guard position, is to perform a *passata sotto* in which you merely BEND THE TORSO VERY LOW and to the LEFT from the guard position. Thrust directly into the LOWER RIGHT CHEST or ABDOMINAL AREA of your opponent. This is a fine attack against an opponent who raises his right arm high in his attack, or otherwise exposes his lower right side. In some instances a left step may accompany the attack.

This movement is also excellent for FAKING a low cut, drawing your opponent's blade low, whereupon you strike for his HAND, FOREARM or HEAD. If he refuses to be drawn low, you may safely risk an attack on his KNEE CAP.

70

A feint, made to look like an actual attack, should affect your opponent's reflexes, causing him to lower an offending guard

A full thrust or cutting attack may be made on your enemy's momentarily open target. Low crouch puts his head in range

71

Keep your free hand in constant readiness to block enemy's blade arm. When it comes in range grab his wrist and thrust

YOUR FIGHTING KNIFE

A stout blade of fine steel is the prerequisite when you go shopping for your knife. The blade should be tough enough to resist most impacts without showing a fixed bend. When severely strained beyond the point of returning to its original position, the blade should bend instead of snapping off. The steel should be hard enough to hold an edge.

Clamp down hard on your opponent's wrist; at the same time
move your body in close and thrust your blade into the target

The knife should be from seven to ten inches in length and resemble
the form of the traditional American Bowie. The handle should be
long enough to fit comfortably and securely in the palm. The weight
of the handle should equal the weight of the blade in order to avoid
the feeling of "blade-heaviness" when the knife is "hefted." The balance
should be near the guard, preferably on the handle side.

Your knife should be equipped with a scabbard that can be secured
to the person in a manner which will make it possible to draw the

73

knife easily and quickly by a natural movement of the hand. The scabbard should be secured vertically on the outside of the right thigh. If this position is impractical because of other gear or heavy clothing, the scabbard may be carried in a horizontal or diagonal position on the front or left front beltline.

Regardless of where the knife is carried, it should be in constant readiness for instant use.

WE REPEAT:

Knife fighting is an ugly business; we hope and pray that you'll never meet an opponent armed with a blade, the look of a madman in his eyes, hatred in his heart, and the momentary lust for YOUR life.

But you might.

And in combat only ONE opponent comes out of a knife fight alive.

If we have succeeded in giving you CONFIDENCE in your own ability with your knife, by these prescribed PRINCIPLES; if we have been able to convince you that your enemy, whoever he is, HASN'T GOT A CHANCE with HIS knife; then we have given you something with which to save your OWN life.

Unarmed Combat

Part III

Unarmed Combat

When Americans settle disputes with their fists—even in barroom brawls—they fight with an admirable, inherent fairness. The tricks of unfair fighting are not in the average American's repertoire; even if he knows them, he will think twice before using them.

On the field of battle there is no time to think twice.

Remember that in combat you are playing for keeps; he who ponders about tactics may not be around to enjoy the next rotation.

Obviously, the man fighting for his life will use every means—fair and unfair—to save it, but the American must be taught "unfair" fighting. On the BATTLEFIELD when his life is in the balance, he CANNOT use effective attacks of hand-to-hand fighting if he DOESN'T KNOW WHAT THEY ARE!

Nor will he be able to protect himself against the onslaught of the dirty fighting he can expect from his opponent.

YOUR BEST DEFENSE IS A GOOD OFFENSE; it must combine your instinct for survival and the practical application of proved principles.

THE STANCE

Your STANCE should enable you to move instantly in any direction. It should make you capable of launching the most effective attack to meet the existing situation.

ONE primary *stance* is recommended:

The knife fighter's stance, with the RIGHT FOOT FORWARD. *Thrusting* or *wheeling* attacks can be launched from this position, as well as a rapid out-of-line pivot in case of a rushing attack.

A diagonal position can be assumed directly from this stance, with your weight on the REAR FOOT, FORWARD ARM raised, as if in protection of the face. Your BODY is REARED BACK from an erect position. From this position an effective kicking attack, from long range, can be launched with the free FORWARD leg and foot. Following the kick you are in a position to launch immediately a back-sweeping elbow, side of the hand, or fist smash.

Use a well balanced knife fighter's stance and you will be in
a position to launch your attack or evade opponent's advance

YOUR PLANS OF ATTACK

Acquire, in the back of your mind, a "library" of PLANS OF ATTACK. These plans are ALL SIMPLE and DIRECT and they will cover a broad selection of situations, logical in individual combat.

Learn to choose the RIGHT attack instantly.

Learn its timely execution.

These PLANS OF ATTACK must be PREARRANGED; they must be outlined and developed in your mind, forming a detailed list from which you may draw instantly when you are confronted with a situation which threatens your life. When the situation confronts you, you will have little time to think it over. A library of PREARRANGED PLANS will be in readiness.

Like swimming, these plans once thoroughly learned, will never be forgotten. Besides, you need not stay in top condition to apply them effectively.

When danger is imminent and you are unarmed, if there is time, look for something to supplement your *natural* weapons—a stick, a stone, dirt, ANYTHING.

At the sight of your enemy coming at you, start to put into action your prearranged *plan of attack*. Assume your proper stance instantly; your choice of attack will depend upon your enemy's stance and the nature of HIS attack.

Launch your prearranged plan of attack the moment he comes within range.

In your plan, simplicity and directness of action will be the keynote of your attack. By TRAINED instinct you will direct your attack in a manner which will exploit any disadvantage you can detect in your opponent. Without a plan and the means to execute it, you are lost. Once the action has started and you find that your original plan is not working, you will automatically switch to another. You will find that this is NOT difficult because ALL of your plans from which you made your initial choice, were SIMPLE and DIRECT.

In the frenzy of a "to the death" struggle, anything short of an absolute blackout blow on your enemy will allow him to remain dangerously fighting for his life—or yours.

Your first step will be to snap yourself into your *stance.*

In an instant you will size up your enemy—his speed, the position of his hands, the way he carries his head.

WITHOUT PREMEDITATION, execute your *plan of attack* the instant he comes within range.

Remember, no one is going to set himself up for you to execute perfectly any routine series of attacks. Explode your whole plan, or any part of it, ALL OVER your enemy in rapid succession.

All of your *plans of attack* are drawn up with one objective in mind —to achieve ultimate victory.

Perhaps you may accomplish this quickly with one direct attack that strikes home . . .

Or it might be a long, drawn out operation . . .

In any case, your *plan of attack* should cover *all* possibilities.

You know that the best way to destroy your enemy is to destroy his primary targets first if you can. In a personal contact with an individual enemy, destroy ANY ONE of his primary targets and victory is yours.

Those primary or high priority targets are:

1. The throat.
2. The groin area.
3. The eyes.

A heavy pounding at ALL OTHER targets will directly or indirectly damage the primary targets and will batter down resistance, allowing OPENINGS for you into his primary targets, which you will immediately attack in a manner prescribed in your *plan of attack*—with hand and fist blows, crushing, gouging, ripping with fingers and thumbs, elbow smashes, knee smashes and knee drops, kicks and stomps with the foot.

From your *stance* you will attack the *targets* described under "TARGETS", with the *weapons* described under "WEAPONS", in a manner prescribed under "ATTACKS."

ATTACKS

Distract and attempt to throw your enemy off balance by heaving a handful of dirt, your cartridge belt, helmet, coins or cigarettes at him. Throw ANYTHING you can get your hands on; throw it the moment he comes into your range.

From the Knife Guard Position

A. *The Thrust Attack.* If your enemy comes at you with his ARMS

If your opponent's hands are low or well into his body, you might try a thrusting attack as soon as he comes into range

LOW or spread out in such a manner as to expose his HEAD, you may start your attack with an exploding STRAIGHT THRUST with your RIGHT, or master hand in the same manner as the execution of a knife thrust. If he *is in range* and is OPEN for such a blow he will not be able to block it. It will land hard enough for you to MOVE RIGHT IN, following your attack through at close range—POINT BLANK range for your most effective blows.

Depending upon the *speed* and *stance* of your enemy, this type of initial attack may be launched in the following manner:

1. Fist exploding on his face.

The thrusting attack. Launch a smashing straight thrust into the face or neck of your opponent. Wheel in with left elbow

2. Fingers extended and joined, thrust into his throat.
3. First two joints of the hand doubled up and thrust into his throat.
4. Fingers extended and spread, ramming them into his eyes.

B. *Follow through of the Thrust Attack.* The instant your initial blow has landed, you *wheel* in close, every weapon you have exploding on every target opening. If there is no target opening, MAKE ONE, keep battering and pounding. It will be impossible for your opponent to protect his COMPLETE body at once. This should give you incentive and confidence. It is not humanly possible for your enemy to protect his throat, groin, eyes, solar plexis, base of skull, kidneys, etc., ALL at the *same time.* You will be forcing the attack, keeping your enemy off-balance and placing him immediately on the defensive; he will be so busy protecting himself that the choice of targets will be yours.

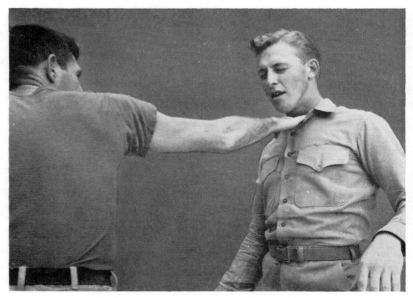

Smash the fingers straight into enemy's windpipe. They may be extended and joined or the first two joints may be doubled

Immediately after a full left elbow smash you are in perfect
position to continue wheeling and smashing at opponent's head

The heavy artillery of the body's natural weapons consists of *both elbows*, the *sides* of *fists*, the *knees* and *feet* and the *forehead*—used as battering rams.

When you close with your enemy, immediately following the right thrust attack, *wheel* or *pivot* in with a left elbow smash, the arms hooked, elbows and fists FLYING. All of the way to the RIGHT, then BACK again, pressing the attack by wheeling and smashing. EVERY full pivot will expose your enemy to a hit from your elbows, fists and the sides of your fists.

The wheel back up to the opponent's jaw is accomplished by a vigorous body pivot, adding power and velocity to the blow

At completion of a left elbow back-smash, your right fist is in position to deliver a solid hook into the groin or solar plexis

If this attack lands successfully and your enemy goes down—*and he is still moving*—prepare to finish him off by planting well placed toe kicks or heel stomps into the following targets:

1. Neck, anywhere, all the way around.
2. Groin.
3. Lower rib region, anywhere, all the way around.
4. All joints.
5. All muscles.

Finish him off with a vigorous stomp or kick to the neck, or a knee drop to the same place.

KNEE DROPS are excellent when your enemy goes down. Merely drop your entire weight, concentrated on ONE of your knees, on any part of his anatomy. Something will GIVE! You may then finish him off with hand blows or gouges and rips to the throat. However, it is SAFER to *kick* and *stomp* when your enemy goes down.

Possibilities

If after your initial attack and follow-through, your enemy is still fighting, you remain *in close* and keep up the assault.

If he grabs your throat, your complete *wheeling* action with a left or right *elbow smash* will break his grip.

If he grabs you *low*, he is exposing his head, neck, etc. Smash at these targets with the sides of the fists, edges of the hands and elbows.

If his head is *high*, smash and thrust at his *throat*, with the hands and edges of the hands.

If he gets a *dangerous* hold on you, SLOW DOWN and grab ONE of his offending fingers and BREAK it, or *crush* his *windpipe* with the thumbs or a blow with the hand or smash at his GROIN. Keep your hands moving in the direction of his *vital targets*. (There are no easily acquired holds that he can get on you which will keep your hands from reaching his groin.) Once you get one of your hands in the vicinity of his throat, eyes or groin, launch your most vigorous attack, smashing, gouging, crushing and ripping.

If he is at any time knocked off balance, leaving you out of arms reach for a moment, kick him, concentrating on the groin, lower rib area and throat area.

If his back is at any time available to you, leap upon it—apply the double-arm strangle hold, wrapping the legs around his waist in a scissors hold. This also will end the fight.

If your two hands are clear, and his ears are in range, slam both hands over his ears as hard as you can. The result will be similar to a blast concussion.

The Wheeling Attack

If a straight thrusting attack is impossible because of an opponent's extended arms, launch a WHEELING ATTACK from your *guard position*. If your opponent is facing slightly to the LEFT, wheel your attack in the direction in which he is *facing*. If he is facing RIGHT, wheel your attack in that direction. This attack will break down his defense and SPIN him around, making any counter attack impossible.

This pivoting *right and left cross attack* was introduced by the late Robert Fitzsimmons who used it to win the heavyweight championship over the late James J. Corbett. It was known as Fitzsimmons' "killing shift."

Colonel A. J. Drexel Biddle's description of this attack clarifies its execution. Here's how it's done:

From a regular boxer's stance (LEFT foot forward) a right hook is aimed at your opponent's chin; at the same time the RIGHT FOOT steps forward, adding speed and force to the blow. Your RIGHT FOOT should advance *outside* of your opponent's LEFT FOOT.

If your right hook failed to land on your opponent's chin, all well and good, the FOLLOW-THROUGH of the blow will have smashed down the enemy's defenses, leaving you LOW and to his LEFT. Instantly rip back up with your whole body, clearing everything with your RIGHT ELBOW, but that LEFT FIST OF YOURS is brought up from the floor and is planted in the SOLAR PLEXIS of your opponent. While this doubles up your enemy, you return to the LOW POSITION and repeat the LEFT HAND PUNCH. This time you can direct it to the point of your opponent's chin. If delivered with KILLING INTENT, this last blow can drive your opponent's jawbones into the base of his skull, resulting in a brain concussion which can cause death.

89

On the battlefield, this same principle can be applied from YOUR guard position (RIGHT foot forward) with NO regard for the right elbow *clearing* before the LEFT fist comes up. Nor is it necessary for you to direct the first left to the solar plexis; a slight lowering of the range into the GROIN, will be more effective for the result you wish to achieve. Keep your body well-balanced with natural foot movements.

If the opponent keeps his face and neck well protected you can batter down his defense by launching the wheeling attack

Smash down his extended arms with full, body-pivoting right
and left hooks. Force the attack by continuing to wheel back

91

Wheel back up with right elbow back smash, directed at any target in range. Follow through with your left fist or elbow

A smashing blow with your left elbow may leave you wheeled
over to your right side. Repeat the attack from left to right

Smash back with the left elbow or edge of left fist. Force an
attack with elbow and fist smashes by pivoting the whole body

94

The Foot Attack

Here is your most effective long range attack. Instead of a straight smashing thrust of the master arm, you rear BACK, shifting the weight on the REAR FOOT, the RIGHT hand raised as if to ward off a blow. As soon as your opponent comes within range, your FORWARD FOOT is thrust forward at your opponent with a FULL snap. The foot, in a HORIZONTAL position, should smash on or below your enemy's KNEE. If his groin is unguarded, you may safely direct your kick into this region.

Whether you hit or miss, follow through with a *wheeling attack*. The arm you had raised before your kick may also be used to smash aside a dangerous blow from your opponent.

You will find that you will actually bounce when you KICK properly. The foot whips out horizontally to its *maximum range*, then whips smartly back. There will be little opportunity for your opponent to grab your leg.

If your opponent is armed with a knife, you will find this foot attack one of the safest and most effective ways of keeping him away from you; if he attempts a cut on your leg, you simply chop his head with a backhand smash.

To stop your opponent at long range, try a foot attack. From
your guard position you will shift your weight to the left foot

96

The shift of weight to the left foot removes your upper torso
from danger and frees your right foot; draw it back and kick

Smash your right leg out, directing the full sole of shoe into
the knee or the upper shinbone of the opponent's forward leg

Follow through with a wheeling attack if your opponent is in
close enough or smash his neck with the edge of your hand

99

WEAPONS

You should supplement your *natural* weapons with anything you can pick up quickly to use as a missile or to hold in your hands. However, the natural weapons, themselves, are numerous and deadly enough when they are properly used.

Here are nature's own weapons:

The Head

The DOME of the FOREHEAD and the BACK of the HEAD are well reinforced as protection against bumping; these areas make won-

If your enemy tries to grasp your neck, you can break his grip instantly by wheeling a left or right cross over his arms

derful BATTERING RAMS. They are used as such by the Danes. Use of the head in this manner is termed the "Danish Kiss" when used to batter in the face of an enemy.

The Elbows

Those elbow bones sticking out when you bend your arms, have been strongly reinforced since childhood. You have crawled on them, rested on them and propped yourself up on them so often that they are tough and hard. When smashed anywhere against an enemy's anatomy, they can do unbelievable damage. The elbows are an effective weapon for use against any target within their range.

As your arm crosses enemy's arms your shoulder muscle, with full body weight behind, bears down on opponent's wrist

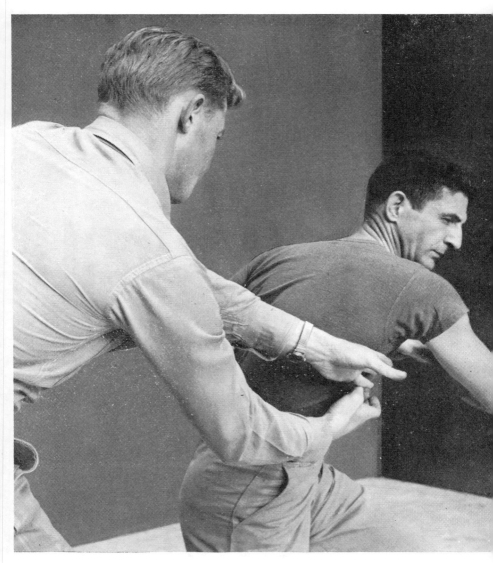

Full body pivot should be used with the right or left cross.
The momentum of the body and its weight will break the hold

As soon as you have broken the hold you may launch your
wheeling attack. Start your offense with a back elbow smash

103

The Hands

The hands themselves are loaded with a fine assortment of ammunition.

With the fingers extended and joined you have the equivalent of a knife point, extremely effective when thrust into vital and soft areas such as the enemy's throat.

By spreading the fingers and thrusting for his eyes you have five small projections that can't miss the target.

For "in-fighting" use your natural battering weapons. Cup the palm of the hand and ram it hard against the opponent's chin

By doubling up the first two joints and thrusting, you deliver a more powerful blow than with the fingers extended and joined. With the finger tips thus PROTECTED, you can strike not only at the throat but at such targets as the *solar plexis, kidneys* and *groin* without fear of injuring the finger tips.

The edge of the hand, fingers extended and joined, is the equivalent of an axe and is used in the same manner. You do not necessarily have to toughen this part of the hand. It is excellent the way it is. You have used your hands all of your life, and that muscle on the edge of the

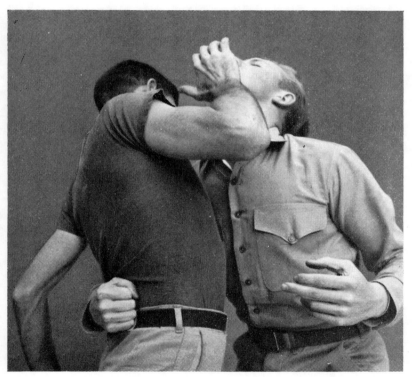

The opponent receives the full impact of the heel of the hand. With this blow you do not endanger your knuckles or fingers

105

hand is tough. Practice in the striking of objects is, of course, good training; it will harden the muscle and develop skill in marksmanship. Learn to strike your target with the muscle and not with your wrist or knuckles. An axe-like blow with the edge of hand can break a neck or rupture a kidney.

The edge of the fist. Note how hard you can pound your fist on a table in this manner; the same blow can be delivered on the neck or groin of an enemy.

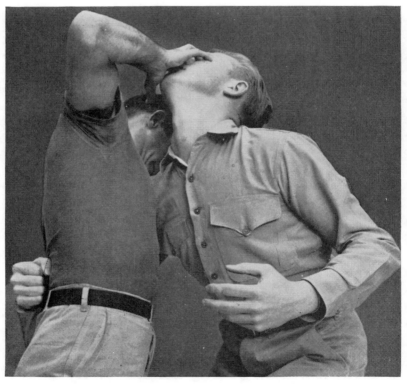

After smashing with the heel of your hand, follow through by curling your fingers over the enemy's face and into his eyes

The heel of the hand. The wrist is locked and firm in all attacks with the hand. This one is an exception. With the fingers extended, bend the whole palm back in the same position as when pushing or leaning palm first, against a wall. The palm in this manner makes a battering ram of your forearm. The natural seat of your palm fits perfectly under the chin of an opponent. When in close, aim an uppercut at your opponent's solar plexis or chest, the heel of the hand will sweep up to chin in a natural arc. The heel of your hand, directly

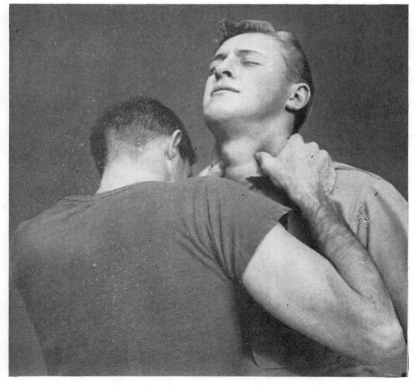

Attack your opponent's throat at the earliest opportunity. With both hands apply thumb pressure to sides of enemy's windpipe

backed by the bones and muscles of the forearm, will connect with the impact of a rock. Close your teeth and try it *gently* on yourself.

Thumbs and Fingers. In tight spots the individual fingers act as probers, gouging and poking at the eyes, the bottom of the throat and under the jawbone. The fingers and thumbs are used for prying at the fingers of the opponent when they are clamped somewhere on your body. Pry one of his fingers loose, clamp your hand around it and

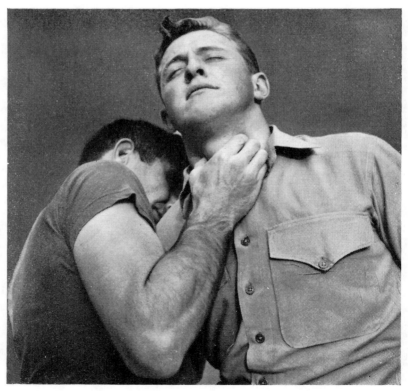

If only one of your hands is free, grasp the windpipe between the fingers and thumb and press in; then snap the trap shut

108

BREAK it. The two thumbs rammed in on both sides of the wind pipe, then snapped together, is a choice way to end an encounter.

The Palm. The results of a punch to your opponent's head in the usual manner are, in many instances, not felt until the next day, but a full resounding slap on the face or base of the skull will rock your opponent right then and there. A good single or double slap across one or both of his ears will drop him on the spot.

If enemy has you in front grip and both your hands are free, slam palms over his ears. Result is like a blast concussion

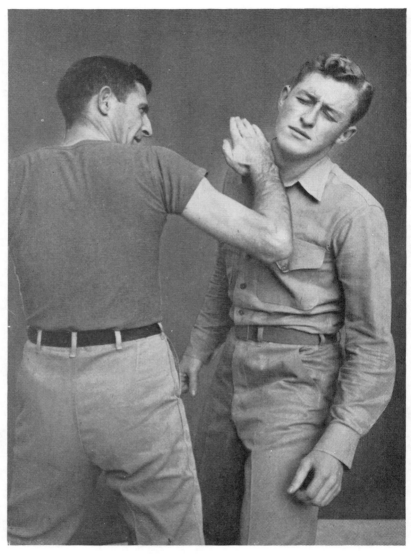

If opponent leaves himself open for blow at throat, smash at
windpipe with edge of hand. Even a light stroke can be deadly

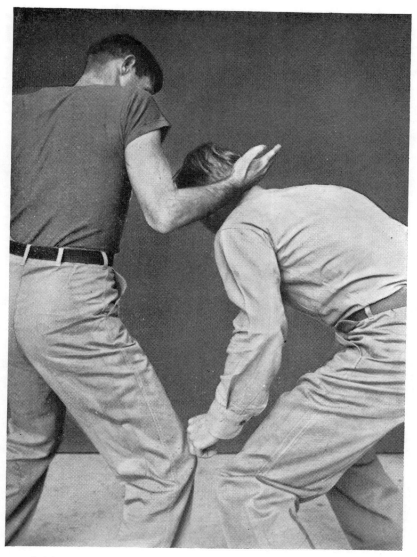

A blow at the base of the skull can break a neck. Nerves or large veins on the sides will paralyze if they are struck hard

The Knees

Two more of nature's battering rams. Use them against the groin, head or anything else that comes within their range. When you are standing over a downed opponent drop your whole weight behind the knee as it falls on some part of his anatomy.

Your knees are powerful battering rams. Use them when you have the opportunity. Opponent's groin is a vulnerable target

The Feet

The broad length of the foot is effective when used as a ram against the opponent's knee in your foot attack. Smash down on his shin bone or shatter his instep if he is standing. *The point of the foot* can be driven into your opponent when it is safe to do so, especially when he is down—to the neck, chest, or joints. Stomp *the heel* down on his instep or use it to kick backwards at his shin, knee or groin.

Notes

A *small rock* will add weight to your clubbing fist.

Any small item, *cigarette lighter, stone,* or *piece of wood* will tighten the muscles on the outside edge of the fist.

A small stick—protruding a bit, front and back—will provide added effectiveness. A small, *tightly rolled piece of newspaper* may be used instead of the stick.

TARGETS

In your initial contact with your enemy there are only two primary targets in which you are interested. Only *one* well placed round, or blow, in either the *throat* or the *groin* will set your enemy up for FINISHING OFF. There are many other targets that you might have to hit repeatedly, all disabling to some degree, but generally speaking, they will be only a prelude to stunning or blacking your opponent out with a blow or blows in one or both of the primary targets.

The Neck

One of your opponent's primary targets is the neck. A severe blow anywhere on the forward half of the neck will cause extreme damage or death. If the blow is delivered at an angle with a back sweep of the edge of the hand, the windpipe will receive a severe jolt or fracture, and the enemy will probably CHOKE to death. A shocking blow at the windpipe delivered in any form was termed the "Black Death" by the late Colonel Biddle. The enemy will either pass out immediately from the shock and pain, choke to death, or remain standing, his face turning darker and darker as he tries unsuccessfully to get air into his lungs. Finally he will pass out.

This angle shot at the throat can damage the vessels which carry the blood to the enemy's head and shock the enemy into immediate unconsciousness by paralyzing the numerous major nerves located in that area. There is NO bone in that whole area to prevent the blow's full effect. If you were fortunate enough to hit so hard from the front, or the back, that you damaged the only bone in the neck, fine. You have finished your job; you have broken his neck.

Attack the front neck area with hand thrusts straight in, finger thrusts, edge-of-hand smashes, (both hands) fist smashes and elbow

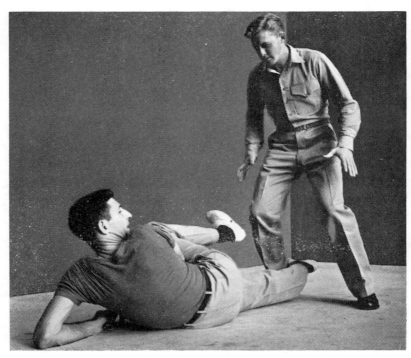

If you are on the ground and the enemy advances, hook one foot behind his ankle and smash his shin with your other foot

smashes. Attack the back of the neck with fist and edge-of-hand smashes.

Groin

Attack your opponent in this area with everything you have; but remember that this is the ONE AREA a man does not have to be TAUGHT to protect. He will instinctively make it very difficult for you to get in a good blow, especially if you try to attack this area by kicking. Don't try a kick at his groin unless you are VERY sure it is unprotected.

Coordination of the two feet is very important; the lower foot hooks ankle at the same time that the other foot smashes out

In an attack from the rear, make approach with left forearm
ready for whipping blow across the front of opponent's throat

Snap forearm hard on enemy's windpipe. Right arm is ready
to lock left forearm in place. Force his midsection forward

117

Whip right arm under left palm, snap right palm under base
of enemy's skull. Lock your muscles in arms, back and chest

The Head

Attack the head with elbow smashes, fist smashes, or a heel-of-hand smash to the chin. Hook your hand behind his head and snap his head forward and come up with a knee smash to his face. When the back of his head is available, smash the edge of the fist or the open edge of the hand across the BASE of the skull. If he is in too close, curl all four fingers into the region of his eyes and start pushing. To force a man to release his grip on you, ram two fingers up into his nostrils and push his nose upward. Your antagonist SHOULD let go!

Rib Cage

When you attack, close in and start your smashing action with elbows, fists and knees; use the head and feet if you can. When your elbows smash against the rib cage ANYWHERE they can inflict severe damage. If you connect around the lower ribs in the front, you will jar the solar plexis nerves. A blow in the lower ribs on the RIGHT SIDE will jar the liver. If you strike the lower ribs in the BACK you will be injuring the kidneys. The whole rib cage is packed with organs and ALL of them will be affected by a severely concentrated blow which lands ANYWHERE in that area. A punch driven into the upper stomach region directly under the center of the chest, will drop your opponent hard and fast. After he drops, a few well placed kicks or stomps or a knee drop in that lower rib area will finish him.

Force the left forearm against enemy's front throat area and as you drop to ground wrap your legs around his midsection

119

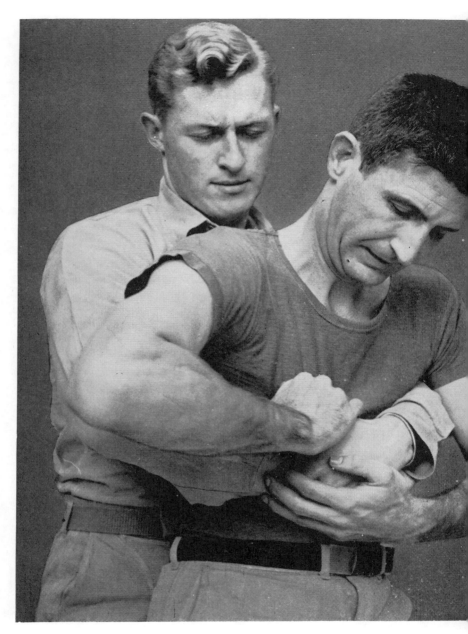

If your opponent gets a bear hug on you from rear and both
of your arms are free, grope for an exposed finger or thumb

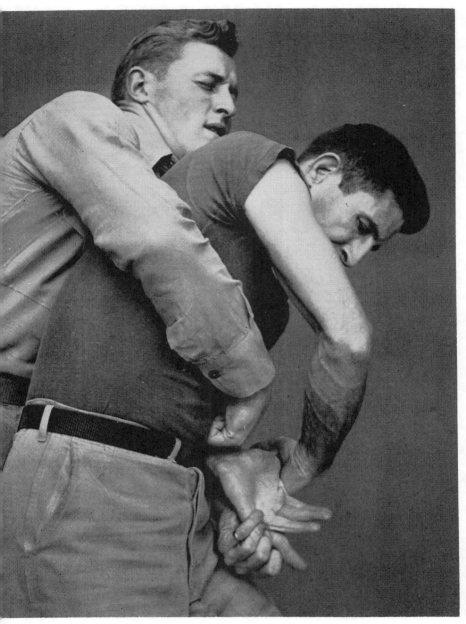

When you find the finger or thumb, peel it free and bend it in opposition to the joint. If you loosen two, spread them apart

If your arms are pinned down in a bear hug, arch the back,
bend forward and apply pressure to your enemy's midsection

122

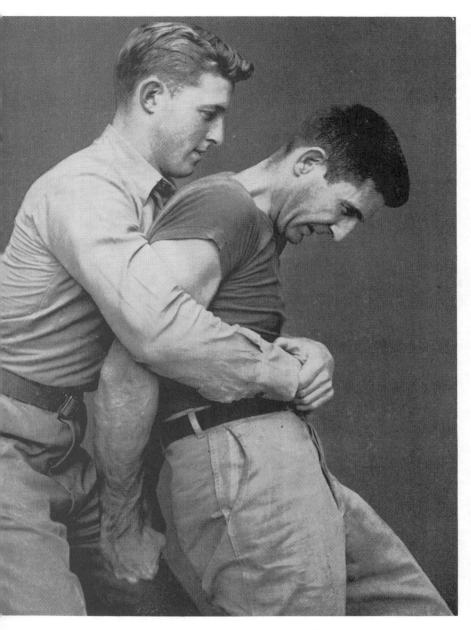

When you release the pressure suddenly you will be creating
a gap wide enough for you to smash your fists into his groin

The Joints

All of the moving parts on the enemy can be placed in one category. If they are small enough to break with your hands. break them. If your opponent gets his hands on you. find one of his fingers and break it by wrapping five of yours around it and bending it in a direction nature did not intend. Larger joints should be attacked with blows. Slam your heel or foot down on his instep or kick at his knee cap until he is down. Then stomp and kick the moving parts. The ankle. knee, fingers. wrist. elbow and. of course. the neck are good stomping grounds. A KNEE DROP in lieu of the kick for the neck joint will leave you out of danger as far as that one enemy is concerned.

Large Muscles

Smash with fists. knuckles. toe kicks and stomps. A good blow will incapacitate the forearms, biceps. calves and thighs.

CONFIDENCE in yourself—the self assurance that you CAN DO IT —is the first requisite; the rest is a matter of KNOW-HOW and PRACTICE. This confidence will allow you to stay LOOSE. mentally and physically. until the moment which necessitates the application of your chosen *plan of attack*. Then HIT FAST and HARD. pressing the attack to its successful conclusion.

124

The Stick

Part IV

The Stick

Years ago the cop who walked his beat, swinging his night stick, knew that it was fine for clobbering drunks and thieves on the head, but it is doubtful whether he realized the versatility of that short length of hard wood he carried. Today, however, there are a number of effective, fighting tricks with sticks. The uses of the stick are worth passing on to you because sometime it may become necessary for you to defend your life with nothing more than your *natural* weapons and any stout stick you might be able to pick up.

The list of common articles, usually available and easily adapted for use as "sticks", is limitless. Swagger sticks, broken broomsticks, mops and shovel handles, snapped-off billiard cues, rungs of chairs or short branches of trees. Ladies in the subways will find a short umbrella or a rolled-up magazine equally effective.

THE SHORT END TECHNIQUE

For the most part, the development of this *short end* technique must be credited to Colonel William A. Kengla, USMC.

Pick up your "stick," whatever it may be, and we'll show you how much damage you can do with it. If you're at home, pull a towel rack off the wall; if you're in jail, pull a bar out of the window. ANYTHING long, stout, hard, about 22 inches in length will do.

Got it?

Good. Here's how you'll hold it:

The Grip

Grab it, just as you would a KNIFE. The fingers are wrapped securely around it, allowing approximately three inches of the stick to protrude OUT IN FRONT of your hand. The remainder of the stick lies along the forearm, forming a straight line from the point to the elbow. Now allow the long end of the stick to drop by your side.

127

The short end technique. Grasp your stick about three inches
below the forward end; the body must be very well balanced

The Stance

Your *stance* may be either that of the boxer (left foot forward) or
that of the knife fighter (right foot forward). However, the left foot
forward, stick in the right hand, is recommended for most situations.

The attack. Your stick performs a piston-like motion as it is whipped up along the forearm and thrust into exposed target

The Attack

ANY ONE of the blows described here will be decisive if planted properly in a vital target area. Your choice of attack will depend upon the situation.

129

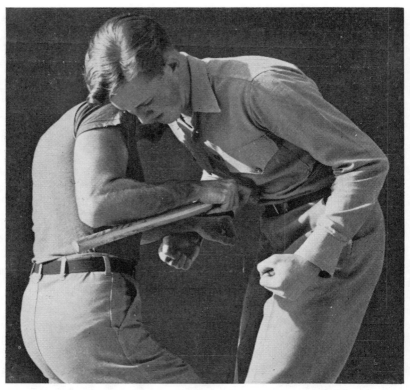

The opponent's solar plexis is your target. The impact is on end of your stick, backed by power of full arm and shoulder

THE SOLAR PLEXIS BLOW is delivered from the boxer's stance, your stick cocked against your forearm, your LEFT foot forward. With a driving, piston-like action of the stick arm, you smash the stick directly into the solar plexis of your opponent. The blow is carried in with additional force by advancing the right foot as you strike. If you CONNECTED, you have succeeded in discouraging your opponent and he will show no more interest in the fight.

However, if you missed or if your blow was blocked, FOLLOW

Your stick will form a bar in a split second if you whip it to
the left and into your left hand with a simple wrist movement

THROUGH by WHIPPING the LONG END of the stick over to your
left side with a single movement of the WRIST. Your LEFT HAND,
PALM DOWN, should be ready to receive. Your stick is now a
HORIZONTAL BAR, gripped in both hands and held at a midsection
level.

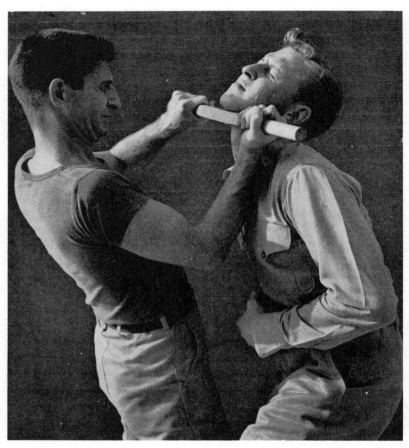

The bar is smashed up under chin with the full power of the
arms and shoulders. Complete smash with full follow through

DRIVE the bar up UNDER THE CHIN of your opponent.

All right, so you missed on the way up—SMASH IT ACROSS THE
BRIDGE of his nose ON THE WAY DOWN. Draw it back to yourself
and smash it straight to his nose, teeth or throat. If your opponent
is still obstinate, MOVE IN.

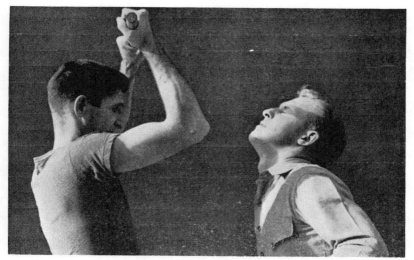

If you missed or merely grazed the chin, leaving bar over opponent's head, you are in a position to continue the attack

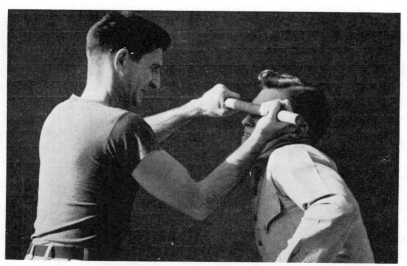

Follow through with a sweeping downward smash. Bring the bar crashing down on enemy's nose if his face is turned up

Bring bar back, close to chest, and prepare for direct smash

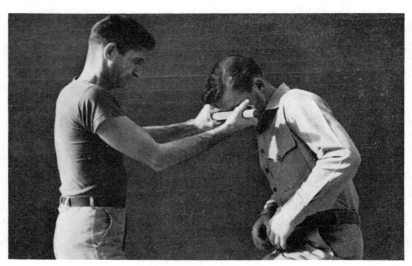

Bar is smashed into enemy's throat, or head between the eyes

134

Grab enemy's shirt and return your stick to forearm position

To MOVE IN, release the left side of the stick and bring it back, along the forearm, into its original position. Now, with your FREE LEFT HAND GRAB A SOLID HUNK OF YOUR OPPONENT'S CLOTHING, somewhere around his right shoulder area and pull him in close. *From now on, wherever he goes, you go!* Start smashing with the SHORT END of the stick—duck low and drive it into his groin, solar plexis or rib area. Strike ANYWHERE, let him have it under the chin if you can get there with it.

135

Crouch low; smash the small end of stick up to enemy's groin

If the groin attack misses, try for your enemy's solar plexis

If you are attacked from the rear while engaging an enemy,
drive the long end of your stick straight back at the offender

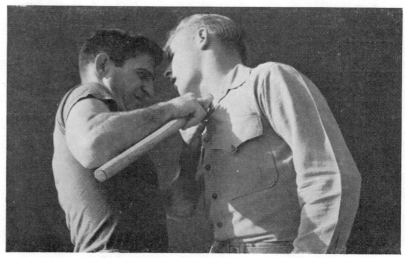

Direct short end of stick to opponent's neck, jaw or temple.
Anywhere the weapon lands will be a painfully damaged spot

If he is blocking your targets, start swinging around the OUTSIDE. Try for his temple, ear, jaw or side of the neck; try for a blow in his lower rib section. ANYWHERE your point lands will be a painfully damaged spot. And a lot of sore spots add up to ONE BIG PAIN. And a painfully bruised body offers LESS RESISTANCE.

Now, you may wish to resort to a PIVOT PUNCH. This outlawed boxing blow is delivered like a right hook to the opponent's jaw, but the point of the elbow, rather than the fist, contacts the target. The upper arm, shoulder to elbow, is too short to deliver this blow effectively without accompanying the blow with a *wheeling body movement*.

The stick is kept along the arm, protecting your elbow as it smashes across your opponent's head after your *right hook swing*. When you deliver this blow, put plenty of "WHEELING BODY" behind it. DON'T PULL YOUR PUNCH!

For the pivot punch, bring the long end of the stick securely along the forearm. Stick will protect your elbow as it strikes

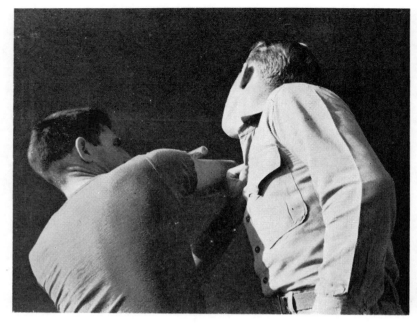

Pivot the body and apply a right elbow smash to enemy's jaw

All right, you missed again. Your blow failed to drop your opponent. Don't worry, you are now in a position to back smash with your right elbow. Make a HOOK with your stick by a slight movement of the wrist; come back across, hooking your opponent's neck with the stick. YOUR LEFT HAND SHOOTS ACROSS IN FRONT OF YOUR OPPONENT, GRABBING THE LONG END OF THE STICK.

This is it, Mac, now you've got it made! Your opponent's neck is now uncomfortably nestled in the DEATH TRIANGLE. The stick behind his neck forms one side, your CROSSED arms on his throat are the other two sides. SNAP THE TRIANGLE SHUT AND SQUEEZE!

Incidentally, this triangle treatment is excellent for curing enemy sentries who have "shouting sickness." You will find that it is a neat, silent way of dropping the sentry from behind. The triangle is simply reversed—the stick flashes in FRONT across his throat, your arms cross on the BACK of his neck. Squeeze until you feel his windpipe close; he can be revived! To kill, squeeze hard!

140

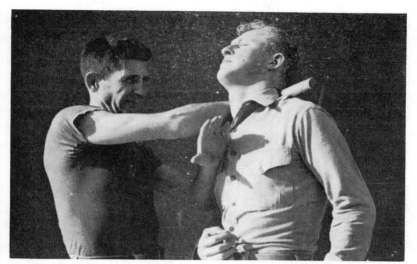

Follow through. Hook is formed with stick around his neck

Arms cross; other end of stick is secured. Snap triangle shut

From this stance you are in a position to attack your enemy
with the short end of the stick or whip it into a bar instantly

To block a kick, whip the long end of the stick across to your left
hand. It has again become a horizontal bar, but instead of bringing
it up to his chin, snap the arms straight down at the oncoming leg.
Aim for the shinbone if possible; then follow up with a chin smash
since the stick is in a position for this movement.

If your opponent attempts to kick, snap your stick over into the bar position. Your feet firmly placed; body well balanced

Snap your arms straight, directing your bar to the shin
of opponent's raised leg; lock arms against power of his kick

Smash your arms out straight against a downswinging blow.
Make use of your feet or knees against any exposed target

Your opponent's overhand or underhand blows may be blocked in this same manner. Smash straight out for the descending arm, or bash aside the upcoming arm. FOLLOW THROUGH AT ANY TARGET OPENING.

145

If your opponent tries an upswinging blow, direct your bar
straight for his wrist or forearm. Draw trunk out of range

At the completion of any block with your bar, follow through immediately with a smash to enemy's forehead, chin or throat

147

THE LONG END TECHNIQUE

Fundamentally, this technique is the use of the stick in the same way you would use a knife.

The Grip

Grasp the stick a few inches from the BACK. This protrusion is a *reserve* for clubbing in close or smashing back at an opponent who may attack you from the rear. The LONG END of the stick is out in front—held out like a knife. The point and the elbow form a STRAIGHT LINE.

The Stance

In COMBAT use the *knife fighter's stance*. Keep the point directed at your opponent and thrust the same way as in knife fighting.

The Targets

Thrust for the throat, face and solar plexis.

The Attack

In combat, if you are otherwise unarmed, find a club and sharpen both ends with a rock. Since you have no cutting edge, direct the whipping action of the club to your opponent's temple, neck, shoulders, joints and muscles. Use the point in full thrusts.

In attacks, from the *long end technique*, a bar may also be formed with a movement of the RIGHT WRIST. Unlike the RIGHT hand grasp used in the *short end technique* where the RIGHT KNUCKLES are DOWN—the fingers UP—the bar formed from the long end stance will have the knuckles on BOTH hands UP.

The bar may be used to smash or the stick may be whipped from either end by releasing the grasp of either hand.

148

The long end technique. Extended long portion is directed at
your opponent. Grasp stick about three inches from the end

Thrust the point of the stick into your enemy's solar plexis.
Your left arm whips back, adding power and velocity to blow

Slash with the long end of your stick in the same manner in which a sabre is used, striking at enemy's joints and muscles

The stick is readily converted to the bar position by flicking
long end over to the other hand with a simple wrist movement

When you assume this position with your bar, you are in an
effective non-aggressive stance, but bar is ready for action

To strike for an exposed target on the opponent's right side,
release the grip of your left hand and strike with your right

To strike at a target on the opponent's left side, release the
right hand and smash across, holding your stick with the left

To attack an enemy from the rear, form hook with the stick
and your arm. Whip the stick across front of enemy's throat

Cross your right arm with your left and grasp the stick with
your left hand. Then snap triangle shut and apply pressure

157

The Come-along. Whip the stick between the legs of offender
and turn it across his thighs. Grab his collar, lift and push

POLICE WORK

While on police duty, you may wish to assume a NON-AGGRESSIVE stance with the stick. Either the SHORT STICK or LONG STICK technique may be used. To achieve a non-aggressive stance with the short stick, grasp it about three inches from the front, allowing the remainder to hang down, pointing to the ground. The short end is now pointing upwards; the fingers grip the stick firmly; the thumb is on the inside, next to the thigh.

This position has an innocent appearance which will enable you to come in close to your suspect without arousing suspicion from him, yet you are in constant readiness to whip the stick up, alongside your forearm to the elbow, and ram its SHORT end directly into the midsection of your suspect if he becomes aggressive. Follow through with your attack as previously prescribed, BUT USE ONLY AS MUCH FORCE AS THE AGGRESSIVENESS OF YOUR SUSPECT DEMANDS.

When you "escort" an offender through a crowd you may wish to move behind him. To move him RAPIDLY and with VERY LITTLE resistance, grasp your stick in the middle; insert it, end first, between his legs and turn the whole stick so that it crosses his thighs; then move it UPWARDS. At the same time grasp the back of his collar with the free hand and PUSH FORWARD. In this manner you will be able to carry him along on his tip toes and completely off balance. This technique is very effective for quick, short trips from curb to wagon or from bar to street.

The use of the stick as a horizontal bar is an excellent technique for the law enforcement officer. He may take his stance in a relaxed manner, his stick horizontal, without conveying the obvious intention of a club raised in a striking pose. YET HE IS IN READINESS TO STRIKE instantly at the offender's hand, forearm, elbow, knee cap or shinbone. The advantage of this technique is the opponent's uncertainty about the direction from which the blow will come. The officer may release either hand and strike with the other. He will do this without premeditation, making his attack without any indication of the side from which it will come.

But whether you're a cop on a beat, a guy walking home from a date late at night, or a mud-sloshin' infantry man, if you're weaponless except for a "stick", these few tips will have given you something to rely on in case of an unforeseen attack. The stick is a versatile weapon and its technique rises far above the common thought of bashing in your opponent's head.

And that's a good defense, too.

Knife Throwing

Part V

Knife Throwing

Only a few of the local boys around Times Square noticed that something was missing. The lights on the Palace Theater sign had gone out. Backstage, the old doorman paused for a last, wistful glance at the darkened house; then he picked up his coat and shuffled through the stage door, locked it for the last time, and stepped sadly into the alley. The Palace had closed; vaudeville had died.

The years which followed left only memories of the acrobats, the ventriloquists, the jugglers, the wire-walkers. But those who mourned vaudeville seldom mentioned one of its most gasp-provoking acts— The Knife Thrower.

The closing of the Palace had been a symbol, it had meant the end of one night stands and split-weeks in the provinces; it had meant that a lot of little boys wouldn't go to bed nights, dreaming about a new ambition—to become knife throwers.

The fascinating desire to throw a pointed knife across a room and make it stick in a solid surface is a natural inclination, but this urge was always stimulated by the glamourous knife throwing act: a roll on the drums, colored spotlights, glistening blades flying through the air, outlining a pert lass in a spangled costume posing against a wooden backdrop. The man in the satin shirt never missed; every knife he threw pingg..ged into the board point-first—and stayed there!

Ever wonder how he did it?

Well, here are the practical principles based on the science of professional knife throwing:

163

THE END-OVER-END METHOD

The END-OVER-END METHOD, used by the professional knife thrower, is the most accurate of the three knife throwing techniques; gratifying results may be obtained quickly and safely by observing its easily mastered principles.

The Grip

Raise the right forearm until it is parallel to the ground. Make a natural fist with the *knuckles* UP. Now place the knife VERTICALLY between the thumb and forefinger. If the knife has only one full cutting edge, this edge should face FORWARD.

Straighten the forefinger, vertically, along the right side of the blade and adjust the knife up or down with your left hand until the tip of your right forefinger is even with the point of the blade. Clamp the blade tightly against the forefinger with the thumb.

Your blade is now VERTICAL to the FOREARM, well secured in a UNIFORM manner, and you are ready for *the throw*.

The end-over-end technique. Line up the knife on the target.
Your arm is extended fully and your blade is held vertically

165

The Throw

From a pistol shooter's position, RIGHT FOOT FORWARD, extend the RIGHT ARM, full length in the direction of the target. Be sure that the knuckles are UP; the blade is VERTICAL; the wrist is STRAIGHT and LOCKED. From this position draw the blade back to the right side of your head. Do NOT develop a BEND IN THE WRIST or in any way change the position of the knife in your hand.

You now have LOADED your weapon, COCKED it, and are ready to FIRE.

Thrust the right arm out, STRAIGHT AT THE TARGET, allowing the blade to leave the hand BY ITSELF. This action is FAST, consequently natural errors can bring about early disappointing results. The following instructions will help to *prevent* or *correct* these errors.

When you thrust your arm at the target, be sure that you are making a FULL THRUST. Do NOT try to apply any WRIST ACTION to "help the blade." The arm when fully extended will stop abruptly, causing a *natural whipping* action of the FIST. This action plus the WEIGHT of the blade, will make the blade leave the hand in a uniform manner EVERY TIME if it is *unassisted* by anything other than VELOCITY.

The foregoing instructions should give you consistent results within the first five minutes of practice, provided of course, that you are throwing from the *correct* distance. When you find this correct range, put a marker on the ground as a guide. Later, with practice, you will SEE the proper range of ANY TARGET, and you will be able to adjust your throws accordingly.

166

Draw your knife well back and keep the wrist straight. Your forefinger should be pressed firmly against the side of blade

167

Thrust your knife arm vigorously straight forward to target. Note that the blade remains at a right angle to the forearm

168

When your arm is fully extended in your thrust, knife leaves
your hand automatically. A wrist snap might result in a miss

Your Guide For Distance

If you are using a blade with an overall length (including handle) of approximately 12 inches, you will stand about *six feet* from your target. If the blade is longer, step back a few inches. At this range, your blade will revolve three-quarters of a full turn from the time it leaves your hand until it strikes the target.

If, after a few perfect throws, the handle of your knife strikes the target in a downward position, you are TOO CLOSE. Move back a few inches.

If your knife consistently strikes the target with its handle facing UP, you are TOO FAR from your target. Move in a few inches.

If you throw according to these instructions you will gain consistent accuracy, your blade entering the target perfectly each time, and you will be controlling the handle well at short range.

After mastering this range, you may wish to double the distance, ADDING ABOUT ONE FOOT to take care of the ADDITIONAL quarter of a turn. Do NOT advance to this range until you are capable of controlling the handle angle with ease at the *shorter* range.

You need NOT have a professional "balanced" throwing knife to achieve satisfactory results; with this technique you can throw practically anything that has a point. Although thrown in the manner prescribed on these pages, such items as ice picks, bayonets or letter openers will *each* demand their proper range.

A balanced throwing knife can be compared to match ammunition, but ANY knife can be thrown with moderately accurate results.

THE POINT-FIRST METHOD

Unlike the theatrical knife thrower, the early frontiersmen and gamblers of the gold rush era threw their knives POINT-FIRST. This method is very effective at close range and the EXACT RANGE is *unimportant* because the knife does not TURN after it leaves the hand.

The Grip

Raise your right forearm until it is parallel with the ground. The fingers are *extended* and *joined*, THE PALM UP, the wrist STRAIGHT. Now place the handle of the blade in the palm of the hand, the point of the blade ON A LINE with the elbow. The handle rests in the palm, forming an extension to the forearm.

Without disturbing this line-up, secure the knife in this position with the THUMB. Merely move your thumb over to the handle and press.

You are now ready for *the throw*.

The point first technique. The knife lies in the palm of your hand, the thumb hooked on the handle, keeping knife in place

171

The Throw

From a LEFT FOOT FORWARD position, draw the knife WELL BACK. Be very careful that you do not upset the ALIGNMENT or the STRAIGHT WRIST. You are now ready to RIFLE the blade to the target with a forward whip of the forearm. SNAP the forearm forward in a direct line to the target, channeling the blade to the target without WHIPPING the FINGERS or the WRIST.

Keep your wrist straight as you draw your knife well back. Elbow and the point of your knife should form a straight line

ALLOW THE BLADE TO LEAVE THE HAND BY ITSELF. Eventually, after a little practice, you will be able automatically to release the thumb pressure at exactly the right moment. Don't try to SHOVEL the forearm straight out from TOO HIGH A LEVEL. This will cut down your velocity. The proper level to obtain maximum results will be approximately eight inches below the belt line.

Your blade is rifled forward in a straight line to the target by the knife hand. Your wrist and fingers should remain firm

DON'T try to draw the forearm straight back horizontal to the ground, and PUSH forward. When drawing the blade well back for the throw, it should be poised about 12 inches behind you, or your right side, your forearm and blade, point down, almost vertical to the ground. From this position you RIFLE the blade straight to the target WITH NO FINGER OR WRIST ACTION. When completing the throw, *follow through* with your arm. In whipping the blade forward your forearm will not be horizontal until the last moment. This follow-through is very helpful in controlling the course of your blade.

Practice

Start your practice throws VERY CLOSE to the target.

If your point shoots UPWARDS, striking with the handle DOWN, you have either WHIPPED with your FINGERS OR WRIST, or you have released the blade TOO LATE.

If your blade strikes with the handle UP, you have released the blade TOO SOON.

If your blade strikes with the handle RIGHT OR LEFT, it is possible that your blade was NOT in a STRAIGHT LINE with your forearm in the beginning.

A HEAVY blade is preferable for this technique; light blades respond too easily to any error you might make.

The blade for POINT FIRST throwing should have a smooth handle. Knobs or other irregularities will hinder uniform throwing.

There are no minimum or maximum ranges for this technique. Your primary object is to make the blade fly through the air STRAIGHT —and with VELOCITY.

When you have mastered "sticking" the blade at a *given* range, you will be able to detect and correct your errors by MOVING BACK BEYOND your effective range. At greater range, slight errors become more obvious.

174

The knife leaves the hand horizontally. Any attempt to guide
your knife with a wrist action is likely to foul your accuracy

THE OVERHAND METHOD

THE GREATEST VELOCITY will be obtained from this technique. The knife shown in the illustrations has completely pierced a truck body and penetrated a one-inch oak panel when thrown at its natural *range*, approximately 12 feet.

The Grip

Grasp your knife with the right hand as you would for a knife fight, and throw it from this grip—the fingers wrapped around the handle, the thumb on top, THE SABRE HOLD.

The overhand method. The knife is held by its handle with the fingers wrapped tightly; thumb is placed on top of the handle

176

The Throw

With your LEFT foot forward, merely throw the knife as you would a baseball, following through with a right step forward and a full natural swing. Unlike the baseball throw, you will add no intentional WHIP. In this technique you will adjust the knife and your DISTANCE to conform with your own NATURAL throw.

If you fail to achieve consistency at your natural range, it is likely that you are adding an unnecessary wrist snap. If you have a NATURAL WRIST SNAP it will be included in your natural throw and will give you no trouble.

The wind-up and position are identical to the baseball throw. Full power and velocity are obtained in this throwing method

177

The handle should slip out of your hand smoothly, the blade making ONE FULL TURN in the air. The 12-inch knife shown in the illustrations will make one turn and strike point first at a 12-foot range when thrown by the author. This same blade, when thrown *naturally*, in the same manner by someone else will make that same turn from anywhere between 11 and 13 feet. YOU WILL HAVE TO FIND YOUR OWN RANGE FOR THE KNIFE YOU ARE USING.

In knife throwing, there is little possibility that you will cut yourself if you are using the proper grip. It is advisable in this technique to have a knife with a smooth handle. If a bayonet is thrown in this manner, many complications can be avoided by holding the handle FLAT in the hand, with the small knob to the LEFT, the edge to the LEFT. The grip is the same, thumb on top. When thrown, the flat sides of the handle will slip along the fingers.

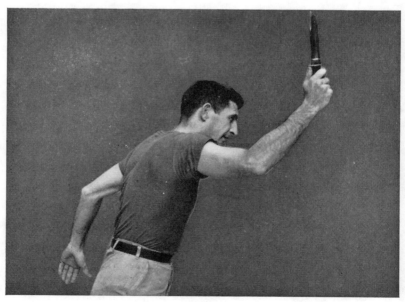

Your natural overhand throw propels the blade to the target. Release the knife without a wrist snap for accurate results

178

If you are unable to achieve consistent results, look to your basic swing as well as to the wrist. The swing should be a full overhand throw with follow-through.

IN THE PRACTICE OF ANY OF THESE TECHNIQUES, safety precautions must be taken. A bad throw means a ricocheting blade— and ricocheting blades are treacherous. Knife throwing can be a lot of fun, but it can be a very dangerous pastime.

The "point first" knife throwing frontiersmen and gold rush gamblers are gone these many years, but the old Palace Theater has opened its doors again to big time vaudeville; maybe the forgotten art of "end-over-end" knife throwing behind the footlights will have a rebirth. Then, too, there's always television . . .

Complete your throw with a full and natural follow-through.
When you have found correct range, concentrate on accuracy

179